Double Stop Musings for Cello

book **one**   by Cassia **Harvey**

CHP139

©2005 by C. Harvey Publications All Rights Reserved.

www.charveypublications.com - print books
www.learnstrings.com - PDF downloadable books
www.harveystringarrangements.com - chamber music

C major

1

Cassia Harvey

©2005 C. Harvey Publications All Rights Reserved.

Double Stop Musings for Cello, Book One

9

Double Stop Musings for Cello, Book One

Across strings

©2005 C. Harvey Publications All Rights Reserved.

Double Stop Musings for Cello, Book One

12

Across strings

13

©2005 C. Harvey Publications All Rights Reserved.

Double Stop Musings for Cello, Book One

14

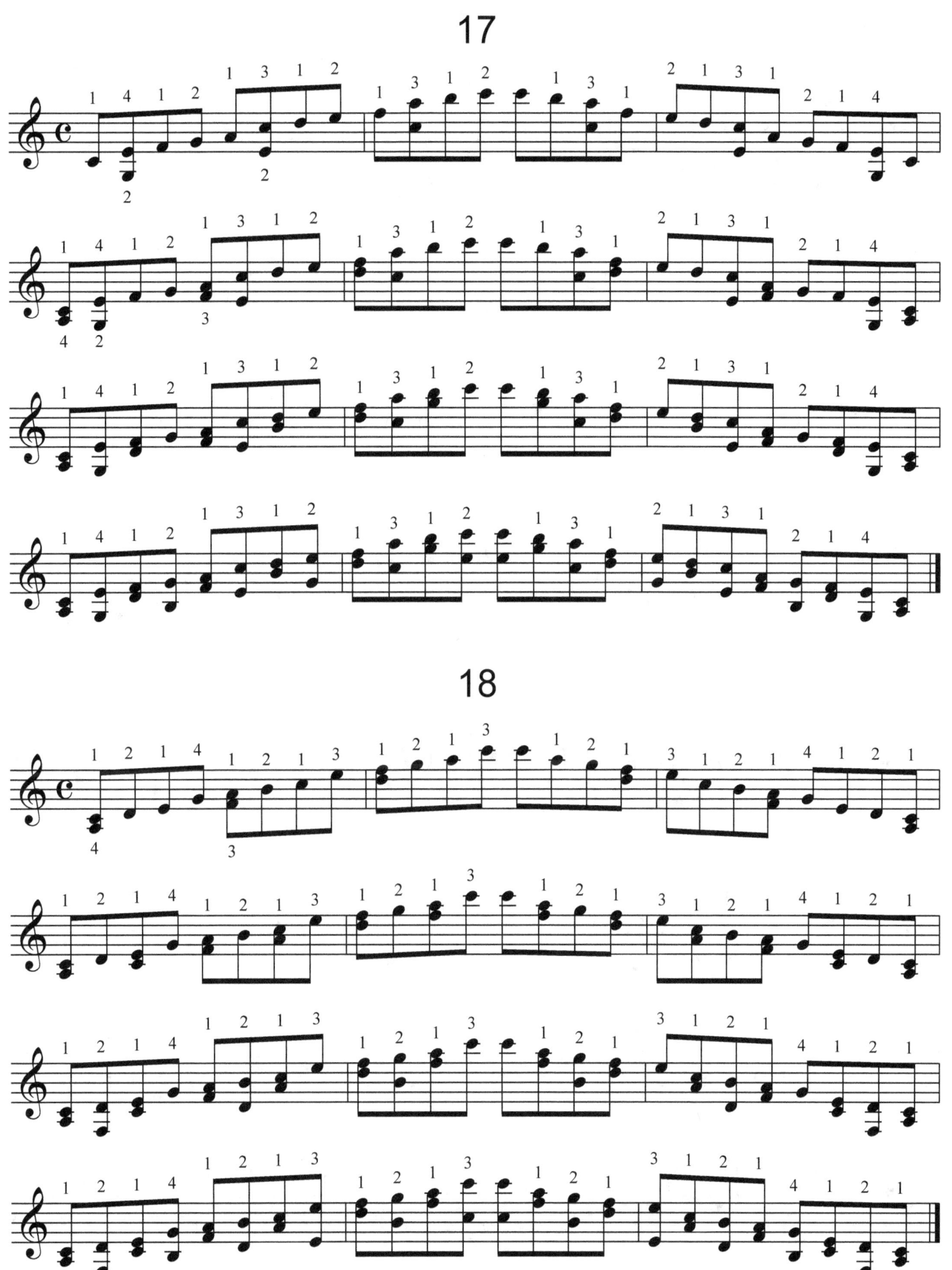

D major

19

20

Double Stop Musings for Cello, Book One

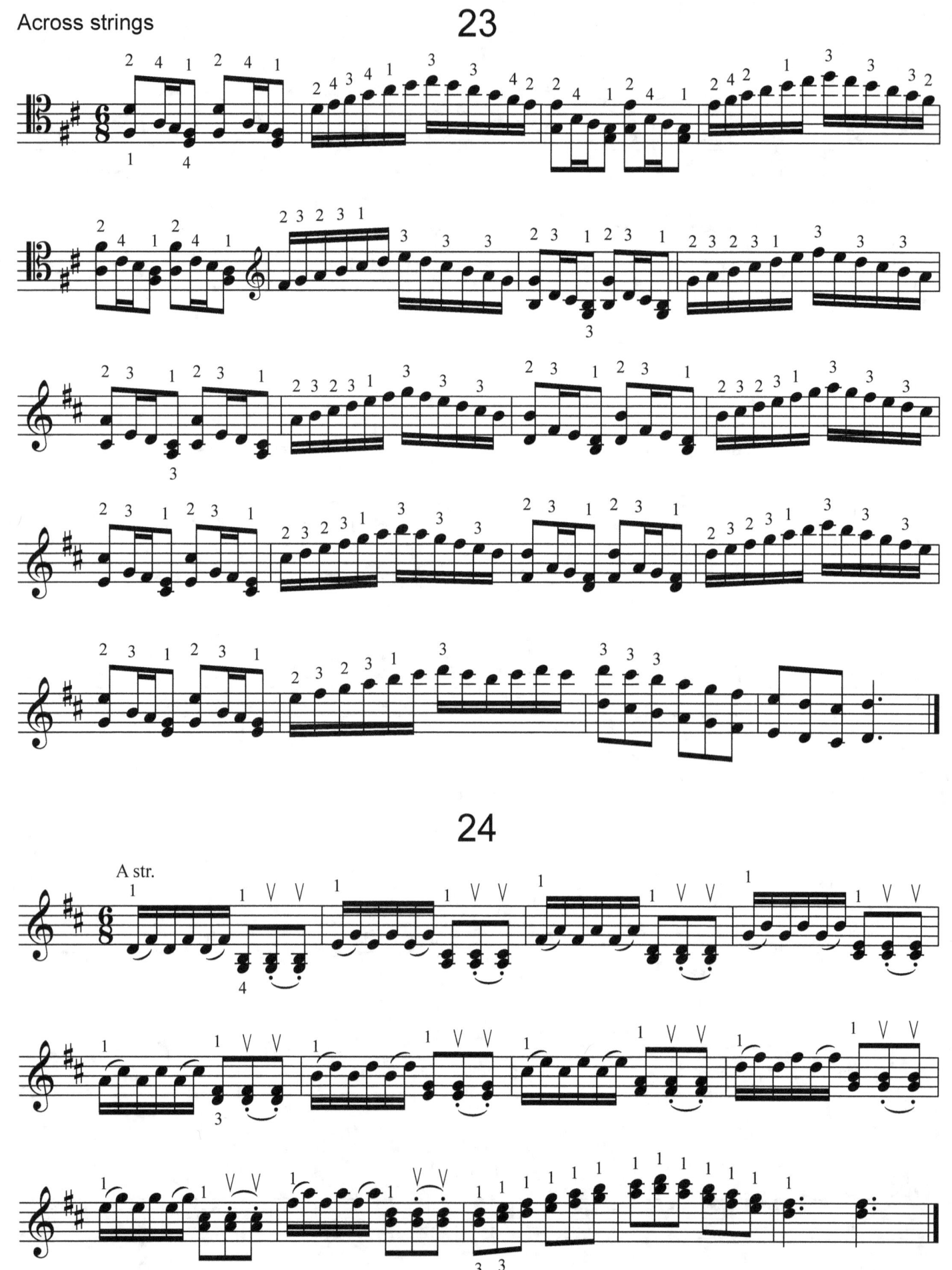

Double Stop Musings for Cello, Book One

29

30

31

Double Stop Musings for Cello, Book One

40

Double Stop Musings for Cello, Book One
25

©2005 C. Harvey Publications All Rights Reserved.

43

Double Stop Musings for Cello, Book One
27

44

45

28

46

47

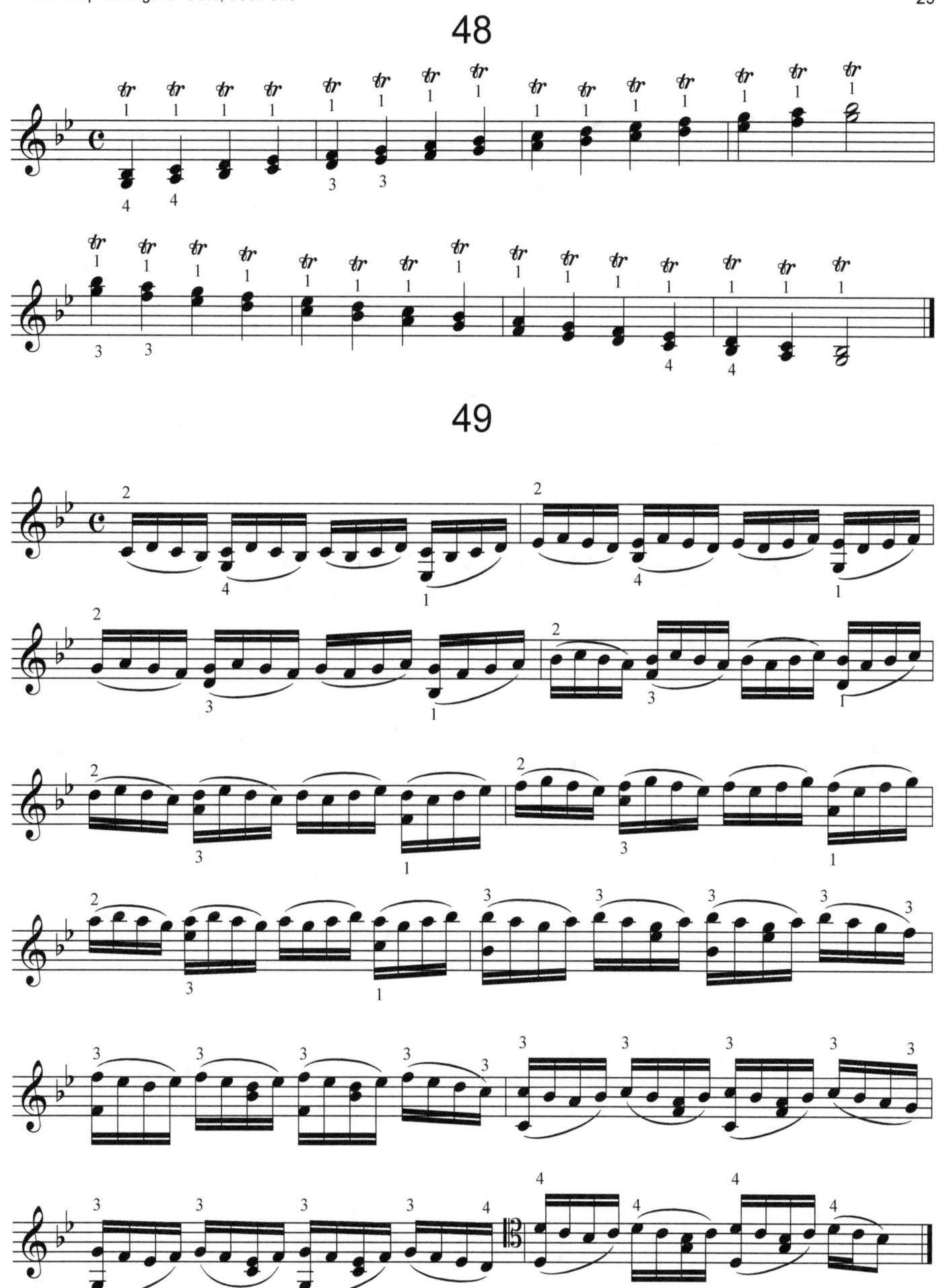

51

www.ingramcontent.com/pod-product-compliance
Lightning Source LLC
Chambersburg PA
CBHW051430070526
44584CB00023B/3657